The United Nations
Leadership and Challenges in a Global World

Economic Globalization and
Sustainable Development

The United Nations:
Leadership and Challenges in a Global World

TITLE LIST

- The Birth of the UN, Decolonization, and Building Strong Nations

- The History, Structure, and Reach of the UN

- The UN Security Council and the Center of Power

- Humanitarian Relief and Lending a Hand

- International Security and Keeping the Peace

- International Law and Playing by the Rules

- Antiterrorism Policy and Fighting Fear

- Cultural Globalization and Celebrating Diversity

- Economic Globalization and Sustainable Development

- Human Rights and Protecting Individuals

The United Nations
Leadership and Challenges in a Global World

Economic Globalization and Sustainable Development

Heather Docalavich

SERIES ADVISOR
Bruce Russett

Mason Crest Publishers
Philadelphia

Mason Crest
450 Parkway Drive, Suite D
Broomall, PA 19008
www.masoncrest.com

Printed and bound in the United States of America.

First printing
9 8 7 6 5 4 3 2 1

Series ISBN: 978-1-4222-3427-3
ISBN: 978-1-4222-3431-0
ebook ISBN: 978-1-4222-8545-9

Library of Congress Cataloging-in-Publication Data
Docalavich, Heather.
  Economic globalization and sustainable development / by Heather Docalavich.
      pages cm. -- (The United Nations: leadership and challenges in a global world)
  Includes index.
  ISBN 978-1-4222-3431-0 (hardback) -- ISBN 978-1-4222-3427-3 (series) -- ISBN
978-1-4222-8545-9 (ebook)
  JZ4972.D627 2015
  338.9'27--dc23
                              2015011492

Design by Sherry Williams and Tilman Reitzle, Oxygen Design Group.
Cover photos: Fotolia/Nobilior (top); Dollar Photo Club/il-fede (bottom).

CONTENTS

KEY ICONS TO LOOK FOR:

Words to Understand: These words with their easy-to-understand definitions will increase the reader's understanding of the text, while building vocabulary skills.

Sidebars: This boxed material within the main text allows readers to build knowledge, gain insights, explore possibilities, and broaden their perspectives by weaving together additional information to provide realistic and holistic perspectives.

Research Projects: Readers are pointed toward areas of further inquiry connected to each chapter. Suggestions are provided for projects that encourage deeper research and analysis.

Text-Dependent Questions: These questions send the reader back to the text for more careful attention to the evidence presented there.

Series Glossary of Key Terms: This back-of-the-book glossary contains terminology used throughout the series. Words found here increase the reader's ability to read and comprehend higher-level books and articles in this field.

INTRODUCTION

by Dr. Bruce Russett

THE UNITED NATIONS WAS FOUNDED IN 1945 by the victors of World War II. They hoped the new organization could learn from the mistakes of the League of Nations that followed World War I—and prevent another war.

The United Nations has not been able to bring worldwide peace; that would be an unrealistic hope. But it has contributed in important ways to the world's experience of more than sixty years without a new world war. Despite its flaws, the United Nations has contributed to peace.

Like any big organization, the United Nations is composed of many separate units with different jobs. These units make three different kinds of contributions. The most obvious to students in North America and other democracies are those that can have a direct and immediate impact for peace.

Especially prominent is the Security Council, which is the only UN unit that can authorize the use of military force against countries and can require all UN members to cooperate in isolating an aggressor country's economy. In the Security Council, each of the big powers—Britain, China, France, Russia, and the United States—can veto any proposed action. That's because the founders of United Nations recognized that if the Council tried to take any military action against the strong opposition of a big power it would result in war. As a result, the United Nations was often sidelined during the Cold War era. Since the end of the Cold War in 1990, however, the Council has authorized many military actions, some directed against specific aggressors but most intended as more neutral peacekeeping efforts. Most of its peacekeeping efforts have been to end civil wars rather than wars between countries. Not all have succeeded, but many have. The United Nations Secretary-General also has had an important role in mediating some conflicts.

UN units that promote trade and economic development make a different kind of contribution. Some help to establish free markets for greater prosperity, or like the UN Development Programme, provide economic and technical assistance to reduce poverty in poor countries. Some are especially concerned with environmental problems or health issues. For example, the World Health Organization and UNICEF deserve great credit for eliminating the deadly disease of smallpox from the world. Poor countries especially support the United Nations for this reason. Since many wars, within and between countries, stem from economic deprivation, these efforts make an important indirect contribution to peace.

Still other units make a third contribution: they promote human rights. The High Commission for Refugees, for example, has worked to ease the distress of millions of refugees who have fled their countries to escape from war and political persecution. A special unit of the Secretary-General's office has supervised and assisted free elections in more than ninety countries. It tries to establish stable and democratic governments in newly independent countries or in countries where the people have defeated a dictatorial government. Other units promote the rights of women, children, and religious and ethnic minorities. The General Assembly provides a useful setting for debate on these and other issues.

These three kinds of action—to end violence, to reduce poverty, and to promote social and political justice—all make a contribution to peace. True peace requires all three, working together.

The UN does not always succeed: like individuals, it makes mistakes . . . and it often learns from its mistakes. Despite the United Nations' occasional stumbles, over the years it has grown and moved for-ward. These books will show you how.

The transition from the post-apartheid era in South Africa is not yet complete: chronic poverty in the mostly black communities is a major problem in the country, as shown in this photo of Kliptown, one of the poorest neighborhoods in Soweto.

CHAPTER ONE

Economic Development

At the United Nations Millennium Summit in September 2000, world leaders agreed to a new set of global development goals. Designed to combat poverty, hunger, disease, illiteracy, environmental damage, and discrimination against women, these Millennium Development Goals address not only human development but provide a framework for the UN's economic development efforts. With a target date of 2015, the eight Millennium Development Goals were designed to be both measurable and achievable. They are listed below.

WORDS TO UNDERSTAND

capital: material wealth in the form of money or property.

collateral: property or goods used as security against a loan and forfeited if the loan is not repaid.

desertification: process by which land becomes increasingly dry.

entrepreneurs: people who set up and finance new businesses to make a profit.

infrastructure: large-scale public systems, services, and facilities of a country or region that are necessary for economic activity.

1. Eradicate extreme poverty and hunger.

2. Achieve universal primary education.

3. Promote gender equality and empower women.

4. Reduce child mortality.

5. Improve maternal health.

6. Combat HIV/AIDS, malaria, and other diseases.

7. Ensure environmental sustainability.

8. Develop a global partnership for development.

Through the Millennium Development Goals, the United Nations aimed to address the many dimensions of poverty, thereby creating a context in which development can be achieved. All eight goals affect economic development, whether helping to alleviate poverty, create a healthy and educated labor force, protect limited resources, or develop a global **infrastructure** for industry and commerce.

Of all eight goals, the last is the one most closely associated with economic development. In order to create a global partnership for development, the United Nations has established seven specific objectives that, when met, should result in such a partnership. Those objectives are as follows:

- Develop further an open trading and financial system that is rule based, predictable, and nondiscriminatory. Includes a commitment to good governance, development and poverty reduction—nationally and internationally.

MORE WORK TO DO

In 2013, world leaders renewed their commitment to achieving the targets set by the Millennium Development Goals. UN secretary-general Ban Ki-moon said that poverty has reached "an unprecedented moment of urgency." As a result, the UN is rethinking the way it is meeting the needs of people. He also said while the MDG program has mobilized groups and individuals to eradicate poverty, climate change is impacting many of the gains made within the last decade. Carbon dioxide emissions are 46 percent higher than they were in 1990, the secretary-general said, and **desertification**, the acidification of the oceans, and land degradation are major problems.

Railways in landlocked countries are important to connect economic activity to worldwide trade networks. Pictured here is a rail line and station with rusted boxcars in Bolivia, a landlocked country in South America.

- Address the least developed countries' special needs. This includes tariff- and quota-free access for their exports; enhanced debt relief for heavily indebted poor countries; cancellation of official bilateral debt; and more generous official development assistance for countries committed to poverty reduction.

- Address the special needs of landlocked and small island developing nations.

- Deal comprehensively with developing countries' debt problems through national and international measures to make debt sustainable in the long term.

- In cooperation with the developing countries, develop decent and productive work for youth.

- In cooperation with pharmaceutical companies, provide access to affordable essential drugs in developing countries.

- In cooperation with the private sector, make available the benefits of new technologies—especially information and communications technologies.

As the MDG deadline approached in 2014, Secretary-General Ban Ki-moon urged global leaders to finish the job and meet the targets. Although the MDGs had "raised awareness, mobilized resources, and helped shape policy .... [transforming] the lives of millions of people," he said more needs to be done.

Pictured here are staff of the UN peacekeeping mission, MONUSCO, distributing school supplies to Congolese children. Inadequate education for all children—covered under MDG 2—is a problem in the Democratic Republic of the Congo, a country whose military conflicts present challenges to economic stability and development.

According to a 2014 UN report on the effectiveness of the campaign, the likelihood of a child dying before the age of five had been reduced by 50 percent; maternal mortality rates dropped by 45 percent; and enhanced HIV treatment had saved an estimated 6.6 million lives. Moreover, 22 million lives had been saved in the fight against tuberculosis, and 3.3 million lives had been saved in the battle against malaria.

"Fewer people are in poverty. More children are in school. We are making inroads in the fight against malaria and tuberculosis. Families and communities have greater access to an improved drinking water source," the Secretary-General said. "We must do more to finish our targets on hunger and chronic child malnutrition. Faster progress is needed to meet the goals of reducing child and maternal mortality and to improve access to sanitation."

As the secretary-general urged action to meet the MDG targets, the entire UN organization began working to reinvent the MDG program and reinvigorate its mission with a post-2015 agenda. Largely focused on sustainable development, new efforts emphasize native solutions to the problems associated with grinding poverty, through programs developed by individual countries and their own civil-society communities. The new agenda also reaches beyond the developing world, and aims to challenge wealthy countries to seek economic strategies that are not damaging to the environment and can be sustained for future generations. In September of 2015, the formal efforts at "rewriting" the goals will begin. Nevertheless, the spirit of the MDGs will remain.

2015 AND BEYOND

Several high-level UN events are planned in 2015 as the Millennium Development Goals program comes to a close and begins to reinvent itself. These include:

- Debate in the General Assembly on implementing the post-2015 development agenda
- Debate in the General Assembly on gender equality and women's empowerment
- Debate in the General Assembly on peaceful settlement of disputes
- Third International Conference on Financing for Development
- Special Summit on Sustainable Development

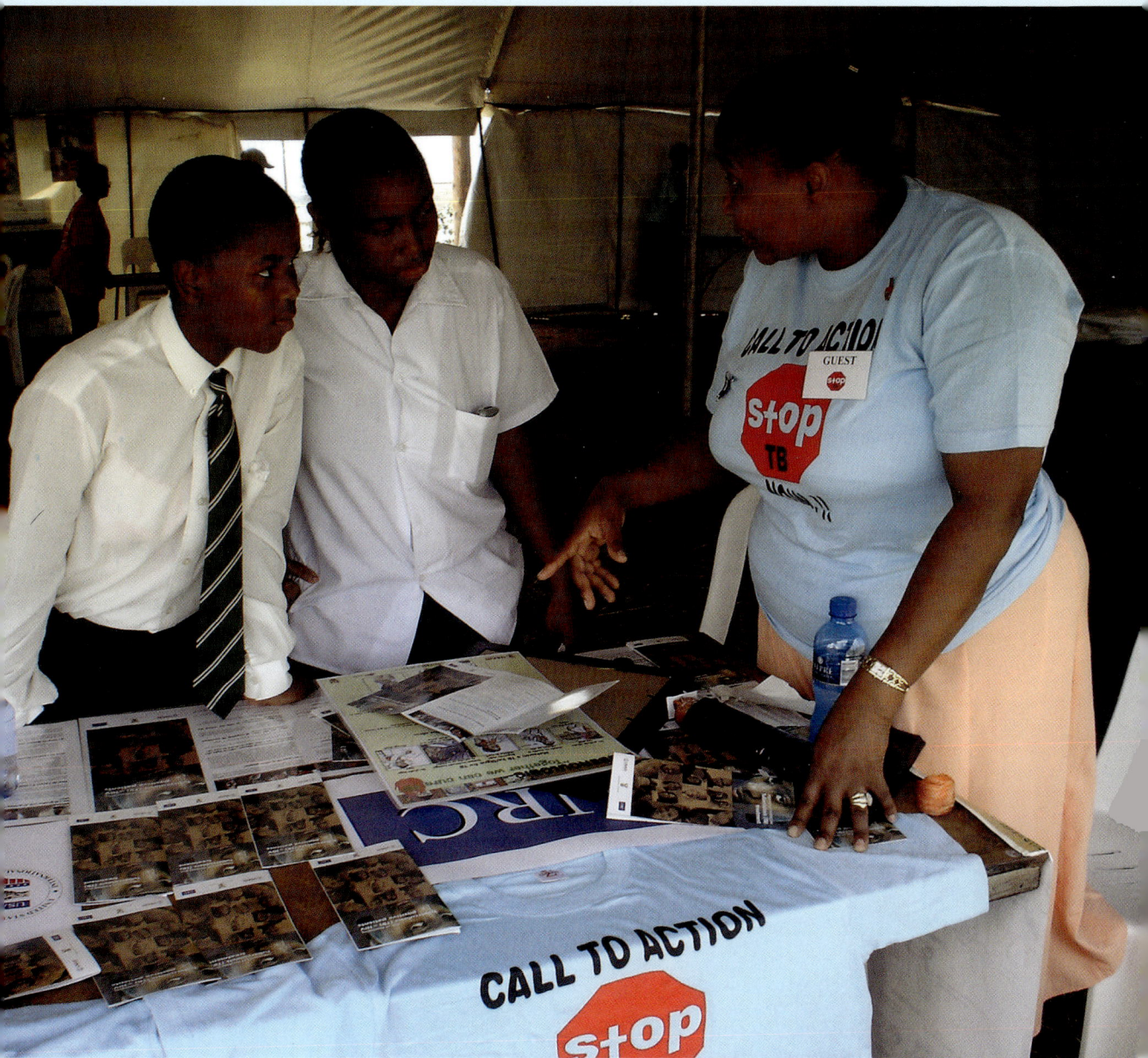

A volunteer speaks to students in 2006 in South Africa under an educational initiative called Stop TB, sponsored by the US Agency for International Development (USAID), intended to inform people that tuberculosis is curable and reduce the spread of the disease.

Official Programs

The United Nations has several official programs designed to assist countries in developing healthy economies. These programs have varying functions and responsibilities, but all share the common aim of achieving the Millennium Development Goals and their related objectives.

The primary UN body concerned with economic development is the United Nations Development Programme (UNDP). The UNDP is the UN's global development network, working to connect countries to knowledge, experience, and resources to help them create their own solutions to global and national development challenges. The UNDP is responsible for assisting developing countries to attract and apply aid effectively. In all areas, the UNDP encourages the protection of human rights and gender equality.

The problem of poor sanitation facilities will continue to attract attention as the UN transforms the MDG program in the post-2015 environment. Here, wastewater in the Indian village of Raika drains in an open road alongside peoples' homes.

Excerpt from the Overview of the "REPORT OF THE UN SECRETARY-GENERAL: A LIFE OF DIGNITY FOR ALL"

Submitted to the General Assembly in September 2013.

Fulfilling our existing commitments and promises on the MDGs must remain our foremost priority. We need to focus on the MDGs that are most off-track and on countries that face the stiffest development challenges, such as the least developed countries. Success on the MDGs will provide a firm foundation upon which to build the next development agenda.

With less than 1,000 days to the 2015 target date for achieving the MDGs, accelerated progress and bolder action are needed in many areas. One in eight people worldwide remain hungry. Too many women die in childbirth when we have the means to save them. More than 2.5 billion people lack improved sanitation facilities. Inequalities between and within countries persist. Our resource base is in serious decline, with continuing losses of forests, species and fish stocks, in a world already experiencing the impacts of climate change.

The Secretary-General's vision for the post-2015 development agenda calls for goals that are measurable and adaptable to both global and local settings and universal—applying to all countries.

The key elements of the emerging vision for the post-2015 development agenda include i) universality, to mobilize all developed and developing countries and leave no one behind; ii) sustainable development, to tackle the interlinked challenges facing the world, including a clear focus on ending extreme poverty in all its forms; iii) inclusive economic transformations ensuring decent jobs, backed by sustainable technologies, and to shift to sustainable patterns of consumption and production; iv) peace and governance, based on the rule of law and sound institutions, as key outcomes and enablers of development; v) a new global partnership, recognizing shared interests, different needs and mutual responsibilities, to ensure commitment to and means of implementing this new vision; and vi) being "fit for purpose", to ensure the international community is equipped with the right institutions and tools to address the challenges of implementing the sustainable development agenda at the national level.

The Secretary-General, in his report, calls on countries and the international community to 1) do everything possible to achieve the MDGs, 2) adopt a post-2015 agenda that is universal and based on sustainable development, 3) embrace a more coherent and effective response to support this new agenda, and 4) provide clarity on the roadmap to 2015.

Source: Press release issued by the UN Department of Public Information, September 2013 (http://www.un.org/millenniumgoals/pdf/SG_Report_MDG_EN.pdf).

Men and women help to clear a street in Carrefour Feuilles after the 2010 earthquake in Haiti as part of the UNDP cash-for-work initiative.

The UNDP helps countries integrate the Millennium Development Goals into their individual national development strategy. The UNDP can help development in these countries to be more effective by ensuring greater awareness of poverty, expanding access to productive assets and economic opportunities, and coordinating aid programs with countries' international economic and financial policies. The UNDP is also working to reform unfair trade practices, provide debt relief, and promote investment to give people of the world's poorest nations access to the global marketplace.

Another important UN program is the United Nations Industrial Development Organization (UNIDO). First organized in 1966, UNIDO is responsible for promoting industrialization throughout the developing world. UNIDO helps to accomplish this goal by working with some of the world's poorest countries and countries with economies in transition to deliver critical skills, information, and technology to promote the growth of employment, a competitive economy, and a sound environment.

Promoting Development

For economic growth to take place, the health of the society as a whole must be strengthened. The United Nations can play an important role in the developing world by simply providing an environment in which development can take place. The UN's many specialized agencies are hard at work in developing nations, promoting peace and stability.

The UN's primary function of promoting peace and security for the people of the world is essential to development, as armed conflict is devastating to most individuals' economic security. Working toward

Trainees learning how to repair heavy equipment at a hands-on UNIDO-sponsored workshop at the Salem Vocational College in Addis Ababa, Ethiopia, in December 2014.

Supporters rally for presidential candidate Francisco Guterres in Timor-Leste (or East Timor), in March 2012. Guterres, the head of the FRETILIN party, and one of the leaders of the armed independence struggle against Indonesia, lost to Taur Matan Ruak in a run-off. Free elections are a positive sign for the new nation, established in 2002.

democracy is another key component in assisting development. By strengthening electoral and legislative systems, improving access to justice, and eliminating governmental corruption, the United Nations can help to provide a more favorable environment for investment and enterprise.

The United Nations also promotes development through its efforts in the area of crisis prevention and recovery. Crises such as the 2004 tsunami in Asia can have a devastating effect on emergent economies. By having resources in place to prevent human-made crises such as war or terrorist attack, and an effective response mechanism to unforeseen catastrophes such as famine, disease, or a natural disaster, the United Nations can protect the often-delicate stability of nations in the developing world.

Lending for Development and Stability

The development banks of today were originally conceived in the years of reconstruction that followed World War II. A group of these development banks—the International Bank for Reconstruction and Development (IBRD), the International Finance Corporation (IFC), the International Development Corporation, the Multilateral Investment Guarantee Agency, and the International Centre for Settlement of Investment Disputes—now make up the World Bank Group. The World Bank is the primary source of funding to poor nations seeking **capital** for development.

Loans are also available from a number of regional development banks, which were established to provide loans and development assistance on a more localized scale. These include the Inter-American Development Bank, the Asian Development Bank, the African Development Bank, and the European Investment Bank. The European Bank for Reconstruction and Development was added in 1991. There are also several subregional development banks, particularly in the Latin American and Caribbean region, as well as several Arab institutions.

The availability of credit to poor nations is critical for the achievement of the Millennium Development Goals. The flow of cash from the wealthier, industrialized nations of the world to the impoverished nations of the

Dr. Sri Mulyani, managing director of the World Bank Group, speaking at a 2012 meeting of the NCDO, the Dutch National Committee for International Cooperation and Sustainable Development. According to their website, the NCDO's Business in Development (BiD) program, "inspires Dutch companies to engage in sustainable business in developing countries."

underdeveloped world is a cornerstone of UN economic policy. New enterprise cannot succeed without money, and this enterprise is essential if the world's poorest countries are to have a position in the global marketplace.

While the UN-affiliated development banks provide loans on the national level, the United Nations also provides for lending on a smaller scale. The United Nations Capital Development Fund (UNCDF) lends small sums to individuals who wish to start or expand small businesses. This has proven to be an effective way to fight poverty and enhance stability. The UNCDF supports small banks in poor countries so they can lend capital to **entrepreneurs** who do not qualify for loans from commercial banks because they lack **collateral**.

Together, these UN efforts work together to build a healthier global economy—which in turn, leads to a more peaceful world. This is not all the United Nations does, however, when it comes to economic development.

CHAPTER ONE

TEXT-DEPENDENT QUESTIONS

1. Describe the general focus of the UN's Millennium Development Goals.

2. Name three successes of the MDGs.

3. Why is working to build democratic institutions important to helping a nation economically develop?

RESEARCH PROJECTS

1. Research a recent natural disaster, such as Typhoon Haiyan in the Philippines, and see what kind of development assistance the UN is providing.

2. Create a table of five to six developing countries, from different areas of the world, and outline the barriers each faces to economic development and what the UN is doing to help each country.

Rapid industrial development in China creates environmental hazards, including air pollution, not just regionally but across the world. Pictured here is an industrial district in Ganjiaxiang, including an oil refinery, a fertilizer plant, and a power plant.

CHAPTER TWO

Sustainable Development

In 1987, the United Nations defined **sustainable** development as "development that meets the needs of the present without compromising the ability of future generations to meet their own needs." The concept states that people can't use up the Earth's limited potential today if they want human life to thrive in the future. Ultimately, no economy can thrive if the environment is unhealthy.

WORDS TO UNDERSTAND

biodiversity: range of organisms present in a given ecological community or system.

biosphere: part of the world, including the air that circulates around and above it, in which life can exist.

consensus: general or widespread agreement among all members of a group.

sustainable: exploiting natural resources without damaging the environment.

The world's natural resources and economy are closely linked. Maintaining healthy forests, such as the one shown here, is important not just for the availability of future products but for the global environment as well.

The origins of sustainable development as a philosophy can be found in the environmental movements of 1960s Europe and North America. As environmental concerns gained increasing attention throughout the decade, governments across the industrialized world began to feel pressure to address the ecological impact of commerce. In 1972, the United Nations held the Conference on the Human Environment in Stockholm, Sweden. This was the first of several international meetings focusing specifically on the environment and development. Each made important contributions to the movement for sustainable development.

The Stockholm Declaration

The Conference on the Human Environment was the first international diplomatic gathering to address human activities in relationship to the environment. The conference was responsible for the creation of the United Nations Environment Programme and the drafting of the Stockholm Declaration. The Stockholm Declaration is the foundation upon which all further sustainable development programs have been based.

The declaration opens with a series of seven proclamations, intended to identify the challenges facing the global community and the work to be done. These read as follows:

1. Man is both creature and molder of his environment, which gives him physical sustenance and affords him the opportunity for intellectual, moral, social and spiritual growth. In the long and tortuous evolution of the human race on this planet a stage has been reached when, through the rapid acceleration of science and technology, man has acquired the power to transform his environment in countless ways and on an unprecedented scale. Both aspects of man's environment, the natural and the man-made, are essential to his well-being and to the enjoyment of basic human rights the right to life itself.

2. The protection and improvement of the human environment is a major issue which affects the well-being of peoples and economic development throughout the world; it is the urgent desire of the peoples of the whole world and the duty of all Governments.

3. Man has constantly to sum up experience and go on discovering, inventing, creating and advancing. In our time, man's capability to transform his surroundings, if used wisely, can bring to all peoples the benefits of development and the opportunity to enhance the quality of life. Wrongly or heedlessly applied, the same power can do incalculable harm to human beings and the human environment. We see around us growing evidence of man-made harm in many regions of the earth: dangerous levels of pollution in water, air, earth and living beings; major and undesirable disturbances to the ecological balance of the **biosphere**; destruction and depletion of irreplaceable resources; and gross deficiencies, harmful to the physical, mental and social health of man, in the man-made environment, particularly in the living and working environment.

Mining has depleted many of the Earth's resources. Open-pit mines, like the Roxia Poieni copper mine in Romania, can cause irreversible damage to the environment.

4. In the developing countries most of the environmental problems are caused by under-development. Millions continue to live far below the minimum levels required for a decent human existence, deprived of adequate food and clothing, shelter and education, health and sanitation. Therefore, the developing countries must direct their efforts to development, bearing in mind their priorities and the need to safeguard and improve the environment. For the same purpose, the industrialized countries should make efforts to reduce the gap between themselves and the developing countries. In the industrialized countries, environmental problems are generally related to industrialization and technological development.

5. The natural growth of population continuously presents problems for the preservation of the environment, and adequate policies and measures should be adopted, as appropriate, to face these problems. Of all things in the world, people are the most precious. It is the people that propel social progress, create social wealth, develop science and technology and, through their hard work, continuously transform the human environment. Along with social progress and the advance of production, science and technology, the capability of man to improve the environment increases with each passing day.

6. A point has been reached in history when we must shape our actions throughout the world with a more prudent care for their environmental consequences. Through ignorance or indifference we can do massive and irreversible harm to the earthly environment on which our life and well being depend. Conversely, through fuller knowledge and wiser action, we can achieve for ourselves and our posterity a better life in an environment more in keeping with human needs and hopes.

There are broad vistas for the enhancement of environmental quality and the creation of a good life. What is needed is an enthusiastic but calm state of mind and intense but orderly work. For the purpose of attaining freedom in the world of nature, man must use knowledge to build, in collaboration with nature, a better environment. To defend and improve the human environment for present and future generations has become an imperative goal for mankind—a goal to be pursued together with, and in harmony with, the established and fundamental goals of peace and of worldwide economic and social development.

7. To achieve this environmental goal will demand the acceptance of responsibility by citizens and communities and by enterprises and institutions at every level, all sharing equitably in common efforts. Individuals in all walks of life as well as organizations in many fields, by their values and the sum of their actions, will shape the world environment of the future.

The declaration then lists twenty-six common principles, defining the obligations of nations and governments in regard to environmental concerns. These form the basis for all further conventions relating to sustainable development. These principles highlight the responsibilities of member states across a broad spectrum of issues. They are presented below.

Principle 1

Man has the fundamental right to freedom, equality and adequate conditions of life, in an environment of a quality that permits a life of dignity and well-being, and he bears a solemn responsibility to protect and improve the environment for present and future generations. In this respect, policies promoting or perpetuating apartheid, racial segregation, discrimination, colonial and other forms of oppression and foreign domination stand condemned and must be eliminated.

Principle 2

The natural resources of the earth, including the air, water, land, flora and fauna and especially representative samples of natural ecosystems, must be safeguarded for the benefit of present and future generations through careful planning or management, as appropriate.

Principle 3

The capacity of the earth to produce vital renewable resources must be maintained and, wherever practicable, restored or improved.

Principle 4

Man has a special responsibility to safeguard and wisely manage the heritage of wildlife and its habitat, which are now gravely imperiled by a combination of adverse factors. Nature conservation, including wildlife, must therefore receive importance in planning for economic development.

Principle 5

The nonrenewable resources of the earth must be employed in such a way as to guard against the danger of their future exhaustion and to ensure that benefits from such employment are shared by all mankind.

Principle 6

The discharge of toxic substances or of other substances and the release of heat, in such quantities or concentrations as to exceed the capacity of the environment to render them harmless, must be halted in order to ensure that serious or irreversible damage is not inflicted upon ecosystems. The just struggle of the peoples of ill countries against pollution should be supported.

Principle 7

States shall take all possible steps to prevent pollution of the seas by substances that are liable to create hazards to human health, to harm living resources and marine life, to damage amenities or to interfere with other legitimate uses of the sea.

The richness of coral reefs like this one at the Palmyra Atoll National Wildlife Refuge, in the middle of the Pacific Ocean, illustrates the importance of safeguarding natural ecosystems.

The BP oil spill in 2010
flooded the Gulf of Mexico
with oil, causing extensive
damage to the gulf's
ecosystem. Pictured here is
the discharged oil spreading
in the water and the boats
letting out "booms" to try to
gather and contain it.

Principle 8

Economic and social development is essential for ensuring a favorable living and working environment for man and for creating conditions on earth that are necessary for the improvement of the quality of life.

Principle 9

Environmental deficiencies generated by the conditions of under-development and natural disasters pose grave problems and can best be remedied by accelerated development through the transfer of substantial quantities of financial and technological assistance as a supplement to the domestic effort of the developing countries and such timely assistance as may be required.

Principle 10

For the developing countries, stability of prices and adequate earnings for primary commodities and raw materials are essential to environmental management, since economic factors as well as ecological processes must be taken into account.

Principle 11

The environmental policies of all States should enhance and not adversely affect the present or future development potential of developing countries, nor should they hamper the attainment of better living conditions for all, and appropriate steps should be taken by States and international organizations with a view to reaching agreement on meeting the possible national and international economic consequences resulting from the application of environmental measures.

Principle 12

Resources should be made available to preserve and improve the environment, taking into account the circumstances and particular requirements of developing countries and any costs which may emanate from their incorporating environmental safeguards into their development planning and the need for making available to them, upon their request, additional international technical and financial assistance for this purpose.

Principle 13

In order to achieve a more rational management of resources and thus to improve the environment,States should adopt an integrated and coordinated approach to their development planning so as to ensure that development is compatible with the need to protect and improve environment for the benefit of their population.

Principle 14

Rational planning constitutes an essential tool for reconciling any conflict between the needs of development and the need to protect and improve the environment.

Principle 15

Planning must be applied to human settlements and urbanization with a view to avoiding adverse effects on the environment and obtaining maximum social, economic and environmental benefits for all. In this respect projects which are designed for colonialist and racist domination must be abandoned.

Principle 16

Demographic policies which are without prejudice to basic human rights and which are deemed appropriate by Governments concerned should be applied in those regions where the rate of population growth or excessive population concentrations are likely to have adverse effects on the environment of the human environment and impede development.

Principle 17

Appropriate national institutions must be entrusted with the task of planning, managing or controlling the 9 environmental resources of States with a view to enhancing environmental quality.

Wind turbines in France on the Rhone River; many countries are fast adopting wind energy as an alternative form of energy, to help slow the effects of climate change.

Sustainable development encourages countries to grow economically without depleting their resources, including farmland, in the process. Pictured here are rows of cabbage at the Wynne Farm, a farming training facility in Kenscoff, Haiti, that teaches about sustainability.

Principle 18

Science and technology, as part of their contribution to economic and social development, must be applied to the identification, avoidance and control of environmental risks and the solution of environmental problems and for the common good of mankind.

Principle 19

Education in environmental matters, for the younger generation as well as adults, giving due consideration to the underprivileged, is essential in order to broaden the basis for an enlightened opinion and responsible conduct by individuals, enterprises and communities in protecting and improving the environment in its full human dimension. It is also essential that mass media of communications avoid contributing to the deterioration of the environment, but, on the contrary, disseminates information of an educational nature on the need to project and improve the environment in order to enable man to develop in every respect.

Principle 20

Scientific research and development in the context of environmental problems, both national and multinational, must be promoted in all countries, especially the developing countries. In this connection, the free flow of up-to-date scientific information and transfer of experience must be supported and assisted, to facilitate the solution of environmental problems; environmental technologies should be made available to developing countries on terms which would encourage their wide dissemination without constituting an economic burden on the developing countries.

Principle 21

States have, in accordance with the Charter of the United Nations and the principles of international law, the sovereign right to exploit their own resources pursuant to their own environmental policies, and the responsibility to ensure that activities within their jurisdiction or control do not cause damage to the environment of other States or of areas beyond the limits of national jurisdiction.

Principle 22

States shall cooperate to develop further the international law regarding liability and compensation for the victims of pollution and other environmental damage caused by activities within the jurisdiction or control of such States to areas beyond their jurisdiction.

Principle 23

Without prejudice to such criteria as may be agreed upon by the international community, or to standards which will have to be determined nationally, it will be essential in all cases to consider the systems of values prevailing in each country, and the extent of the applicability of standards which are valid for the most advanced countries but which may be inappropriate and of unwarranted social cost for the developing countries.

Principle 24

International matters concerning the protection and improvement of the environment should be handled in a cooperative spirit by all countries, big and small, on an equal footing.

Cooperation through multilateral or bilateral arrangements or other appropriate means is essential to effectively control, prevent, reduce and eliminate adverse environmental effects resulting from activities conducted in all spheres, in such a way that due account is taken of the sovereignty and interests of all States.

Principle 25

States shall ensure that international organizations play a coordinated, efficient and dynamic role for the protection and improvement of the environment.

Principle 26

Man and his environment must be spared the effects of nuclear weapons and all other means of mass destruction. States must strive to reach prompt agreement, in the relevant international organs, on the elimination and complete destruction of such weapons.

UN Industrial Development Organization's director-general, Li Yong (right), talking at the 2014 sustainable industry summit Global South-South Development Expo, sponsored by the Organization of American States (OAS). Increasing cooperation between developing countries in the global south is an important part of development strategies, especially in the post-2015 MDG environment.

In the decades that followed the Stockholm Declaration, other steps were taken to address environmental concerns within the context of economic development. In 1986, the United Nations appointed a World Commission on Environment and Development to research important areas of environmental damage around the globe. Led by Norway's prime minister, Gro Harlem Brundtland, the commission conducted its research and reported its findings along with some proposed solutions. Officially titled Our Common Future: Report of the World Commission on Environment and Development,

EARTHWATCH

The Stockholm Conference was the first time that world leaders drew attention to the need to protect the environment and to help people bolster their living conditions through sustainability. The Stockholm Declaration was signed by both industrialized and developing countries.

the Brundtland report brought the idea of sustainable development to the attention of the global community once more and called for international cooperation to combat growing environmental problems.

The Rio Earth Summit

The United Nations held the 1992 Rio Summit in hopes of building upon the foundation laid in the Stockholm Declaration. Public awareness and debate around environmental issues peaked with a number of new agreements dealing with a wide variety of issues, including **biodiversity** and climate change.

A series of twenty-seven principles were proclaimed at Rio with the goal of establishing a new international partnership through the creation of new levels of cooperation among nations, to produce international agreements

The world's nations met in 1992 in Rio de Janeiro to establish an international partnership to protect the Earth's environment.

that respect the interests of all people and protect the best interests of the world's environmental and economic systems. The Rio Declaration created a framework of action for sustainable development in the twenty-first century that eventually became known as Agenda 21. The United Nations also formed the Commission on Sustainable Development (CSD) to monitor implementation of agreements reached in Rio.

Rio +10 and +20

In May 2000, environmental ministers from all over the world met in Malmo, Sweden, to review important and emerging environmental issues and to plan for the future. This led in August 2002 to the World Summit on Sustainable Development (WSSD), held in Johannesburg, South Africa. This conference, also known as "Rio+10," focused on new scientific evidence of global environmental change. In the Summit's Political Declaration, world leaders promised to commit themselves to working together, united by a common determination to save our planet, promote human development, and achieve universal prosperity and peace. Leaders also pledged to speed up efforts to accomplish the time-bound, socioeconomic, and environmental targets contained in the implementation plan. In 2012, a third summit, Rio+20, was held. During the conference, countries renewed their commitment to sustainability. Those who attended called for a wide range of actions, such as making the UN Environment Programme stronger.

Although the United Nations has made considerable progress in promoting sustainable development worldwide, much debate remains— not only among nations, but among varying interest groups, industries, and nongovernmental organizations (NGOs)—as to the best way to realize these goals. While the Johannesburg Declaration made a strong stand for sustainable development, some key areas were not addressed due to a lack of clear **consensus**. Most notably, summit negotiations were stalled in three prominent areas: agriculture subsidies, energy interests, and exemptions from some environmental protections for the poorest countries.

Despite these issues, Agenda 21 is an ongoing UN plan that builds the global economy by protecting the environment. And with a renewed commitment to sustainable development in the post-2015 development agenda and the transformation of the MDG program, Agenda 21's goals are sure to be strengthened.

A panel on incorporating sustainability into economic development policies was held in Doha, Qatar, in April 2012 in preparation for the Rio +20 summit to be held in June of that year.

CHAPTER TWO

TEXT-DEPENDENT QUESTIONS

1. How many proclamations are included in the Stockholm Declaration? How many principles?

2. What is a biosphere?

3. What year was the Rio Summit held?

RESEARCH PROJECTS

1. Imagine you are a representative from a developing country at the Rio Earth Summit. What proposals would you support? What parts of the Rio Declaration might you not agree with? Write a short report on why you feel this way, citing research from other sources to back you up.

2. Create a public service announcement (PSA) showing how your school can become more sustainable. The PSA can be in the form of a newspaper ad, poster, computer slide-show presentation, or audio/visual production.

Protests in 2010 over Hazelwood Power Station, a coal-based power plant in Victoria, Australia. Generating power in coal-fired facilities contributes greenhouse gases to the atmosphere, which aggravates climate change.

CHAPTER THREE

Agenda 21

Agenda 21 is the UN blueprint for sustainable development. A comprehensive plan to achieve sustainable development globally, nationally, and locally, Agenda 21 describes the responsibilities of the United Nations, individual governments, and major groups in every area in which humans impact the environment. It was so-named because of its significance as a model for economic growth in the twenty-first century.

WORDS TO UNDERSTAND

demographic: characteristics of a human population.

ecotourism: form of tourism that strives to minimize ecological or other damage to areas visited for their natural or cultural interest.

free-market economy: economic system in which businesses operate without government control in matters such as pricing and wage levels.

globalization: process by which social institutions become adopted on a worldwide scale.

indigenous: native born to a region.

Development of Agenda 21

The full text of Agenda 21 was drafted through a painstaking process of negotiation that began in 1989. Revealed at the 1992 United Nations Conference on Environment and Development (the Rio Earth Summit), 179 governments voted to adopt the program. Outlined in the Rio Declaration, Agenda 21 is comprised of twenty-seven principles designed to address every area of economic development.

Agenda 21's forty chapters are divided into four sections. The first addresses social and economic issues such as combating poverty, changing consumption habits, population and **demographic** dynamics, promoting health, promoting sustainable settlement patterns, and integrating environment and development into decision-making. The second section is concerned with conservation and management of resources for development, including atmospheric protection, combating deforestation,

Agenda 21's second section is concerned with protecting the world's forests. Overharvesting lumber has devastated forests in some regions, such as those shown here Tasmania, Australia.

THE U.S. and AGENDA 21

Some U.S. officials and residents have been wary of Agenda 21, although most Americans—85 percent—don't know what it is. In fact, at the 2012 Republican National Convention, opponents persuaded the GOP to pass a resolution against Agenda 21 "as erosive of American sovereignty." A small group of Americans believe Agenda 21 is a conspiracy to take away their guns and to turn the United States into a Soviet-like state.

protecting fragile environments, conservation of biodiversity, and control of pollution. Section three seeks to strengthen the roles of children and youth, women, NGOs, local authorities, businesses, and workers. Section four describes the specific means by which the plan should be put into practice.

In December 1992, the UN General Assembly established the Commission on Sustainable Development (CSD) to oversee the implementation of Agenda 21 and report on the progress being made on the global, national, and local level in meeting its objectives. The commission is composed of fifty-three members elected to three-year terms and meets once a year for a period of two to three weeks. It reports to the Economic and Social Council and, through it, to the Second Committee of the General Assembly.

The Economic and Social Council elects CSD members from among UN member states. Thirteen members are elected from Africa, eleven from Asia, ten from Latin America and the Caribbean, six from Eastern Europe, and thirteen from Western Europe and other nations. One-third of the members are elected annually, and outgoing members are eligible for reelection. Other countries, UN organizations, and accredited intergovernmental organizations and NGOs are welcome to attend CSD sessions as observers.

The CSD has several important functions. Originally, it was designed to have a rather limited role in evaluating progress toward the implementation of Agenda 21. However, in recent years it has been assigned greater importance in developing policy and working as a liaison between governments, the international community, and the major groups identified in Agenda 21 as key actors outside the central government with a significant role to play

MAASAI WOMEN BUILD HOMES

In Kajiado, Kenya, Maasai women honed their skills building homes because of the initiatives fostered by Agenda 21. Five hundred members of eleven women's groups were trained in home-building technology.

in the move toward sustainable development. These groups include women, youth, **indigenous** peoples, NGOs, workers and trade unions, business and industry, scientists, and farmers.

In 1997, the UN General Assembly held a special session to review five years of progress toward the implementation of Agenda 21. In this session, known as Rio+5, the Assembly acknowledged that progress was "uneven" and identified troubling new issues including increasing **globalization**, widening inequalities in income, and a continued deterioration of the global environment. A new General Assembly resolution was drafted promising further action.

A UN-organized World Summit on Sustainable Development (also called the Earth Summit) took place in Johannesburg, South Africa, from August 26 to September 4, 2002, to further discuss sustainable development issues. Held ten years after the World Summit in Rio de Janeiro, the Earth Summit gathered a number of leaders of nations, businesses, and NGOs. Once again, a resolution was drafted promising further action in implementing Agenda 21. Critics, however, drew attention to the inability of the United Nations to enforce the provisions of Agenda 21. They also cited a lack of commitment from the world's wealthiest nations. U.S. president George W. Bush did not attend the Johannesburg Summit; many who were there booed U.S. Secretary of State Colin Powell over the absence of the U.S. president.

The Rio+20 Summit, held in 2014, focused on sustainable development and how it relates to green economies and the eradication of poverty, and how best to create an institutional framework for sustainable development. The conference focused on creating decent-paying jobs, energy, sustainable cities, food security, and various sustainable practices.

During the conference, countries renewed their commitment to sustainability. Those who attended called for a wide range of actions, such as making the UN Environment Programme more effective.

Indigenous farmers in Bolivia learn about organic farming techniques and sustainable use of resources with the help of computer technology.

Agenda 21 in Action

Agenda 21 was intended to outline appropriate action at the international, national, regional, and local levels. Many governments have legislated or advised that local authorities take steps to implement the plan locally, as recommended in chapter 28 of the document. The resulting programs are known as "Local Agenda 21." Agenda 21 also urges action by NGOs. This provides a framework for action when there is little or no political will to make sustainable development a priority. The tiny nation of Slovenia in Central Europe, provides an excellent example of how Agenda 21 was meant to function.

In 1990, Slovenia, in south-central Europe on the Adriatic Coast, became a nation in transition as it shifted from a communist country to an independent state with a **free-market economy**. Although the changes in social and

The Sunga Wastewater Treatment Plant pictured here used a "constructed wetland" to help process, filter, and recycle used water in the town of Madhyapur Thimi, in central Nepal. It was built with the financial help of UN-HABITAT's Water for Asian Cities Programme, the Asian Development Bank, and Water Aid.

economic systems present a unique opportunity for the implementation of sustainable development, the Slovene government has been slow to enforce existing environmental legislation or to work more aggressively toward sustainable development out of fear that it could slow economic growth.

Agenda 21 for Slovenia was born in response to fears that the Slovenian government was not aware of the importance of environmental issues and of the commitments made in Rio. Coordinated by Umanotera, the Slovenian Foundation for Sustainable Development, the project was initiated in 1995 with a brief survey of Slovenian NGOs to determine how familiar they were with key international principles of sustainable development.

The first national-level workshop, held later that year, welcomed twenty-four members from nineteen Slovenian NGOs and a number of observers from the Slovene government. Workshop participants identified key environmental problems and obstacles to sustainability in Slovenia. These problems occurred within three dimensions of activity: cultural, political, and economic. It was determined that "solutions" to specific problems in one area simply emerged as new problems somewhere else—or in the future. So to harmonize necessary changes with principles of sustainable development, reform would be approached on all three levels simultaneously, with full awareness of the laws applying to interrelationships within the system.

Several additional workshops were held dealing with problems on the local level before a second national workshop was convened. The second national workshop produced a strategy for sustainable development titled "Agenda 21 for Slovenia: A Contribution of Non-Governmental Organizations." The document was based on the discussions held in the workshops, with an in-depth analysis of the present state of development in various sectors of Slovenia.

Ljubljana, Slovenia, the capital city; this small nation uses the principles of Agenda 21 to help it implement sustainable development strategies.

The Julian Alps in Slovenia, which extend into northern Italy, are one of Europe's most important Alpine habitats.

Although this process was neither initiated nor sponsored by the government, the resulting development blueprint has prompted governmental action. Pavel Gantar, Slovene minister of environment, announced that the ministry would use the document in drafting a national environmental protection program. Zare Pregelj, chairman of the Parliamentary Council on Environment and Infrastructure, proposed that parliament study the plan and commission a more in-depth study on transition toward sustainable development.

Agenda 21 for Slovenia has already seen some modest successes. For example, NGOs in Maribor have worked to ease traffic and reduce pollution by making the city bicycle-friendly, modeling it on a project in the nearby Austrian city of Graz. Nature conservation programs are also showing positive results. Skocjanski Zatok on the Adriatic Coast, one of the only wetland environments in Slovenia, is now turned into a protected area.

One of the recommendations from the Agenda 21 for Slovenia workshops was to develop a series of small pilot projects. Such projects demonstrating principles of sustainable development in practice offer an opportunity to build momentum and overcome resistance to change. As a result, a three-year project was designed to "adopt" an existing corporate farm and aid it in its conversion to organic farming and **ecotourism**. Not only can it serve as a demonstration farm, but it can also offer valuable knowledge and experience gained in the process of transition.

Slovenia's magnificent mountains give way to coastal environments on the Adriatic Sea in Europe. One of Slovenia's only wetlands, Skocjanski Zatok, pictured here, has been put under protective status.

The spirit of Agenda 21 as a means to provide a healthy and prosperous future for generations to come can be summed up in this statement by Agenda 21 for Slovenia:

> Respecting the natural and cultural properties of our land, we can reach a considerably higher degree of development and quality of life. A combination of traditional approaches and modern technology will assist us in living within the limits of environmental space for Slovenia and the planet Earth. . . . With this document, we hope to present an optimistic concept of a human society as a self-regulating system, capable of balancing itself with nature while not having to sacrifice economic development or quality of life. Outdated social and economic structures will be the only necessary "sacrifices" in this process.

CHICAGO GOES GREEN

The UN touts Chicago's "Urban Greening Initiative" as an Agenda 21 success story. The city passed two ordinances requiring trees to be planted in all new residential and commercial developments. Moreover, the city began requiring that all parking lots have at least 10 percent green space, and that nonprofit groups could purchase for $1 tax-delinquent land if they used the property as open space. The ordinances aimed, in part, to make Chicago a more aesthetically pleasing city.

CHAPTER THREE

TEXT-DEPENDENT QUESTIONS

1. What are the main goals of Agenda 21?

2. Explain the difference between a free-market economy and communism.

3. How does Chicago's "Urban Greening Initiative" relate to the goals of Agenda 21?

RESEARCH PROJECT

Research whether your community or state is doing anything under Local Agenda 21. Create a list of those projects and discuss with your class how they relate to the goals of Agenda 21.

Through the UNDP, AusAID funds fisheries development through micro-finance in northeast Sri Lanka in the aftermath of the 2004 tsunami.

CHAPTER FOUR

Development Programs

The UNDP, or United Nations Development Programme, is the United Nation's primary body providing economic development. Established in 1965, the UNDP was created to unify the operations of the Expanded Program of Technical Assistance and the United Nations Special Fund, which continued as separate components of UNDP until full unification in 1971. The UNDP is the chief source of technical assistance to developing countries, with most of its aid coming in the form of consultants' services, equipment, and fellowships for advanced study abroad.

Thousands of projects in areas as diverse as resource planning, training institutes, the application of modern technology to development, and the building of the economic and social infrastructure are supported by the UNDP. It also dispenses UN special purpose

WORDS TO UNDERSTAND

advocacy: active support for a cause or position.

demobilizing: discharging personnel from the armed forces and sending them home.

electoral: relating to elections.

eradication: the total destruction or removal of something.

funds for resource exploration, combating desertification, and technology development, as well as working with UN-associated agencies involved in development activities.

The UNDP is funded by voluntary contributions from UN members. The agency not only provides its own assistance but assists developing countries to attract and use aid effectively. Its various programs focus on work helping countries develop—and share—solutions in three areas of critical importance:

- sustainable development

- democratic governance and peacebuilding

- climate and disaster resilience.

The UNDP is also responsible for generating the Human Development Report (HDR). The HDR was first launched in 1990 with the objective of putting individuals back at the center of the development process in terms of economic debate, policy, and **advocacy**. The idea was to go beyond income when evaluating the level of people's long-term well-being.

Evaluating Human Development

The HDR is an independent report commissioned by the UNDP. However, it is the work of a selected team of leading scholars, development practitioners, and members of the Human Development Report Office. The report is translated into more than a dozen languages and issued in more than a hundred countries annually.

Each year the report focuses on a specific topic or theme in the current development debate, providing important analysis and policy recommendations. People around the world have implemented the report's proposals. The value of the HDR and its approach is shown by the publication of national human development reports at the national level in more than nearly 150 countries.

The HDR has developed four separate indexes to evaluate human development. These statistical rankings—the Human Development Index (HDI), the Gender-Related Development Index, the Gender Empowerment Measure, and the Human Poverty Index—are often important in determining a country's need for foreign aid. The HDI is a comparative measure of

The Mudeirej Bridge in Lebanon, in 2011. It was partially destroyed in the 2006 war between Hezbollah militia and Israel. USAID helped to rebuild it.

poverty, literacy, education, life expectancy, and other factors for countries worldwide. It is a standard means of measuring well-being, especially child welfare. The United States ranked fifth on the HDI in 2013, up from tenth for 2005. Above the United States, from first are Norway, Australia, Switzerland, and the Netherlands.

The compilation of these statistics and reports by the UNDP is critical to evaluating development and progress around the globe. The data collected assists in creating development agendas and priorities that direct international attention toward the economic, social, political, and cultural issues that oppress people in the world's developing nations. The HDR is an important tool for policy analysis that works by identifying inequities and measuring growth.

Democratic Governance and Peace-Building

Democracy is good for the economy—and democratic governance is essential for "an enabling environment" for the realization of the goals and, in particular, the elimination of poverty. At the same time, poor countries are unusually vulnerable to violent conflicts and can be more severely affected by their aftermath. Having good governance structures in place helps in peacemaking during and peace-building after conflicts, even if political infrastructure has been weakened or even destroyed during civil upheavals and war.

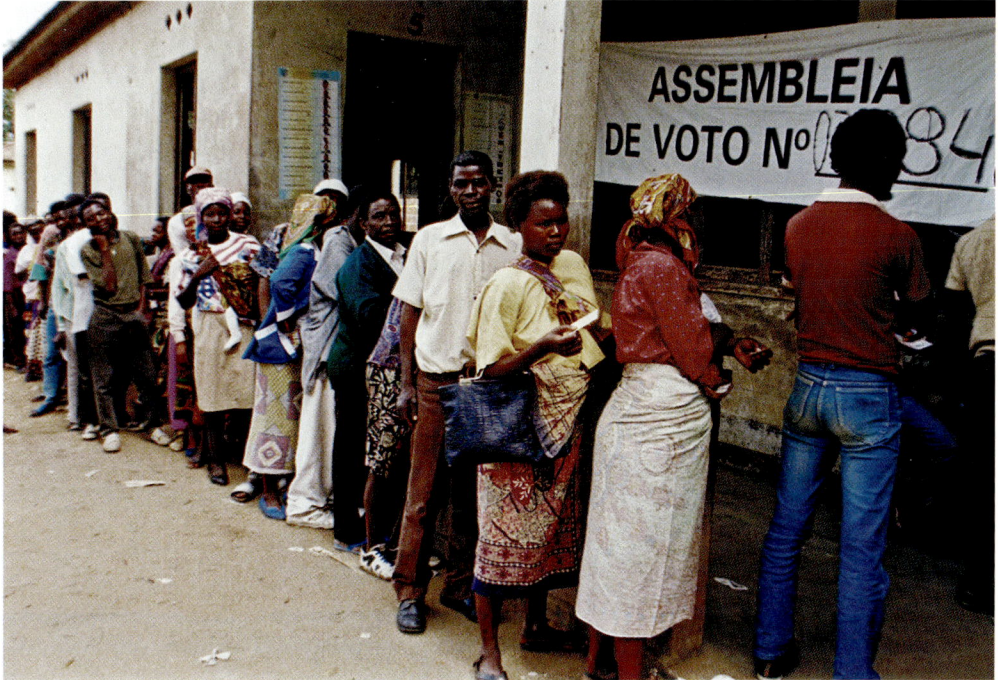

Mozambicans wait to vote in a UN-assisted election in 1994; democratic governance helps to establish conditions for continued economic growth.

The critical importance of democratic governance and peace-building in the developing world was highlighted at the Millennium Summit of 2000, where the world's leaders pledged to "spare no effort to promote democracy and strengthen the rule of law, as well as respect for all internationally recognized human rights and fundamental freedoms, including the right to development." By improving the quality of democratic institutions and processes, the United Nations hopes to stave off civil conflict, reduce poverty, better protect the environment, and promote human development.

The UNDP works to develop institutions and processes that are more responsive to the needs of ordinary citizens, especially the poor. The UNDP brings people together—within nations and internationally—to promote participation in government and improve accountability and effectiveness at all levels. Countries receive assistance to strengthen their **electoral** and legislative systems, improve access to justice and public administration, and develop an enhanced ability to deliver basic services to those most in need.

BATTLING MALARIA

With the help of the UNDP, malaria cases in Bolivia have been drastically reduced. Since 2010, the Malaria-Free Bolivia project has been raising public awareness about the mosquito-borne disease and helping doctors eradicate the illness. People are told how to use mosquito netting and when to stay indoors. The project's goal was to eliminate the most-deadly strain of the virus by 2015. The project was so successful that in 2013 only nine people in the thirty-six communities covered by the program had contracted the most dangerous form of malaria.

The UNDP provides support and assistance to countries that require aid in instituting electoral processes. By supporting sustainable development, as well as electoral processes and institutions that allow all citizens to elect their representatives freely and hold them accountable for commitments, a more favorable environment is created to attract foreign aid and investment.

In societies undergoing rapid change as an effect of globalization, political transition, or civil conflict, well-organized administrative services can simplify the implementation of national development plans. The UNDP helps to build public service structures that are cost-efficient and results-oriented, and that answer to the citizens they are intended to serve. Honest management of public financial resources constitutes one of the most fundamental responsibilities of government. Preventing and combating corruption is a major challenge for many governments in the world, particularly those in developing countries and for economies in transition. Minimizing corruption is critical to stimulating investment, reducing poverty, and promoting sustainable development.

The UNDP's support for democratic governance and poverty reduction has given it a well-established track record. From Mozambique and Afghanistan to Guatemala and Albania, the UNDP has played a major role in helping countries develop a viable agenda for economic development by promoting the rule of law and fair governance, working toward justice and security, **demobilizing** soldiers, reducing the flow of small arms, eliminating environmental hazards such as land mines, and putting war-affected people back to work.

Sustainable Development

In accordance with the Millennium Development Goals, developing countries worked to create their own national poverty-reduction strategies based on local needs and priorities. The UNDP speaks for these poor nations and helps to make their efforts more effective through providing a greater voice for poor people, creating greater access to productive assets and economic opportunities, and coordinating national poverty programs with international economic policies. And as the MDG goals are transformed in the post-2015 development environment, the goal of poverty **eradication** will be strengthened through a sustainable development strategy.

The UNDP sponsors pilot projects, connects developing countries to the world's best practices and resources, promotes the importance of women in development, and brings governments, civil society, and outside investors together to better coordinate their efforts. Such actions to reform trade, grant debt relief, and promote investment all help support national poverty reduction and make globalization work better for poor people. Besides its advocacy work, the UNDP focuses on policy advisory services that seek to ensure that both national and global trade, debt, and capital flow policies function on the basis of human development concerns.

PROTECTING SAMOA'S FORESTS

In 2011, the UNDP instituted a four-year program to address sustainability issues in Somoa, and protect the inland forests on the island. With the help of the agency, fourteen villages cultivated a variety of native trees and plants to replace stands of forests damaged by logging, deforestation, and storms. Local youth planted the seedlings, not only helping the environment, but also providing them with much-needed jobs.

Climate and Disaster Resilience

Natural disasters—such as the December 2004 tsunami that devastated Asia—can erase decades of development and further ingrain poverty and inequality. And as climate change advances, natural disasters, as well as their effects, will continue to threaten countries across the world, especially developing nations.

With a network of global partners, the UNDP develops and shares innovative approaches to disaster relief and post-crisis recovery. The UNDP has worked to provide quick and effective response to natural disasters. When short-term humanitarian aid is phasing out, the UNDP provides sustainable recovery initiatives by directing attention to disaster relief and preparations for the rebuilding process. Such crisis response is at the core of the UNDP mandate for poverty elimination.

The December 2004 tsunami brought a tidal wave of new poverty to Banda Aceh in Indonesia.

CHAPTER FOUR

TEXT-DEPENDENT QUESTIONS

1. Name the three areas of importance to the UNDP.

2. How does the UNDP support countries devastated by natural disasters?

3. How did the UNDP help cure the water woes in the Afghan village of Jukna?

RESEARCH PROJECTS

1. Choose a country that is ranked as one of the world's poorest nations according to the Human Development Index. Create a journal entry describing what your day might be like if you lived there. Would it make a big difference whether you were a boy or a girl? Why or why not? Back up your answers with facts about the country and its daily life.

2. Research the various projects of the UNDP and create a photographic collage showing how the agency helped people in those localities.

An immense chasm lies between the lives of people in poor areas and the lives of those who live in wealthier regions. Pictured here is Valhalla Park in Cape Town, South Africa, February 2013, one of the poorest neighborhoods in the city.

Financing Development

As the United Nations renews its commitment and strategy to reduce poverty post-2015 and reworks the Millennium Development Goals, a primary concern is how such development can be financed. The gap between the poorest and the richest nations of the world has continued to widen. Various aspects of international policy require reform in order for developing countries to benefit from the process of globalization.

Recent changes have been made to address the ever-growing need for development dollars. The first steps toward reform came from the International Conference on Financing for Development, which was held in March 2002 in Monterrey, Mexico.

Known simply as the Monterrey Conference, this first UN-hosted conference to address key financial and development issues attracted fifty heads of state or government, over two hundred high-level ministers, leaders from the **private sector**, and senior officials of all

WORDS TO UNDERSTAND

constitute: to be a part of a whole.

multilateral: many sided.

private sector: ordinary people who are not formally involved with government.

ratify: officially approve.

the major intergovernmental financial, trade, and economic organizations. The far-reaching plan of action drafted at this conference is known as the Monterrey Consensus, in which countries with developed, developing, and transition economies pledged to undertake important actions in domestic, international, and systemic policy matters. In 2008, a follow-up conference was held in Doha, Qatar. In Doha, developed countries renewed their commitments to the levels of Official Development Assistance they agreed to prior to the worldwide recession began in 2007.

Official Development Assistance

Official Development Assistance (ODA) is still the largest source of aid to underdeveloped countries. ODA has its roots in the aftermath of World War II. In 1944, the forty-four Allied nations gathered at the United Nations Monetary and Financial Conference in Bretton Woods, New Hampshire. This conference led to the establishment of the International Bank for Reconstruction and Development (World Bank) and the International Monetary Fund (IMF). These still **constitute** some of the largest sources of ODA.

ODA is money to be used for development. Although most often the aid will be in the form of a loan, the loan is made more on the basis

THE FOUNDING AND MISSION OF THE FDO

Following the Monterrey Conference, the United Nations established the Financing for Development Office (FDO). The mission of the Financing for Development Office, according to its website, is:

to provide effective secretariat support for sustained follow-up within the United Nations system to the agreements and commitments reached at the International Conference on Financing for Development, as contained in the Monterrey Consensus, as well as financing for development-related aspects of the outcomes of major United Nations conferences and summits in the economic and social fields, including the development goals set out in the United Nations Millennium Declaration.

Headquarters of the West African Development Bank in Lomé, Toga, in western Africa. As the entity focused on development for the West African Economic and Monetary Union, it is funded by member banks, international agencies, and foreign governments.

of need than credit worthiness. The loan part of the aid received will have low interest terms and a long repayment period. To qualify as ODA, at least a quarter of the money received will never have to be paid back.

Governments give this money through individual countries' international aid agencies, through institutions such as the World Bank, and through individuals involved with NGOs such as Care International or Oxfam. The wealthiest UN member states have pledged to make specific amounts available as ODA in order to meet the Millennium Development Goals.

The major institutions involved in ODA funding are the IMF, the World Bank, the World Trade Organization, and the UNDP. These institutions regularly meet to discuss the implementation of the Monterrey Consensus and projects on financing for development. In addition, the Financing for Development Office brings together experts from the official and private sectors, as well as academia and civil society, to examine issues related to the mobilization of resources for financing development and poverty reduction.

Multilateral Institutions

The World Bank, IMF, and WTO are **multilateral** institutions that provide development assistance. Developed in response to the need to rebuild after the devastation of World War II, these institutions now provide assistance to impoverished, war-torn, and disaster-stricken nations all over the world.

The World Bank is a crucial source of financial and technical assistance to developing countries. It is not a bank in the regular sense, since it is made up of two separate development institutions—the International Bank for Reconstruction and Development (IBRD), which is owned by 188 UN-member countries, and the International Development Association (IDA), owned by 173 member countries. Each of the World Bank's institution plays a different but vital role in the effort to do away with poverty and improve living standards worldwide. The IBRD focuses on loans to middle income and creditworthy poor countries, while the IDA focuses on grants to the poorest countries in the world. Together the two institutions provide low-interest loans, interest-free credit, and grants to developing countries for education, health, infrastructure, communications, and many other important purposes.

The IMF is the central institution of the international monetary system, the system of international payments and exchange rates among national currencies that enables business to take place internationally. It aims to prevent crises in the system by encouraging countries to adopt sound economic policies; it is also an actual fund that can be accessed by members needing temporary financing to address economic problems. Headquartered in Washington, D.C., it is governed by its membership of 188 countries.

The UN cannot meet its development goals without funding from its richest members.

THE IMF EXPLAINED

According to the IMF's articles of agreement, "The purposes of the International Monetary Fund are:

i. To promote international monetary cooperation through a permanent institution which provides the machinery for consultation and collaboration on international monetary problems.

ii. To facilitate the expansion and balanced growth of international trade, and to contribute thereby to the promotion and maintenance of high levels of employment and real income and to the development of the productive resources of all members as primary objectives of economic policy.

iii. To promote exchange stability, to maintain orderly exchange arrangements among members, and to avoid competitive exchange depreciation.

iv. To assist in the establishment of a multilateral system of payments in respect of current transactions between members and in the elimination of foreign exchange restrictions which hamper the growth of world trade.

v. To give confidence to members by making the general resources of the Fund temporarily available to them under adequate safeguards, thus providing them with opportunity to correct maladjustments in their balance of payments without resorting to measures destructive of national or international prosperity.

vi. In accordance with the above, to shorten the duration and lessen the degree of disequilibrium in the international balances of payments of members.

The Fund shall be guided in all its policies and decisions by the purposes set forth in this Article."

The port of Singapore, one of the most active in the world. The WTO and other international economic institutions work to expand international trade; in doing so, they hope to increase economic growth for all countries.

The World Trade Organization (WTO) deals with the rules of trade between nations at a global or near-global level. Made up of members from 160 different countries, its primary purpose is to help trade flow as freely as possible without creating undesirable side effects. In part, that means removing barriers to free trade. It also means ensuring that individuals, companies, and governments know what the trade rules are around the world, and to provide the world with stable and predictable trade practices.

The WTO is an important negotiating forum in which representatives from member nations try to resolve the trade problems they face with each other. Everything the WTO does is the result of negotiations. The majority of the WTO's current work comes from the 1986–1994 negotiations called the Uruguay Round and earlier negotiations under the General Agreement on Tariffs and Trade (GATT). Once a set of negotiations ends and the nations reach an agreement, each individual government must **ratify** the new laws. Such trade negotiations try to respect the nation's other treaty obligations, including UN resolutions.

Most of the WTO's members are developing countries. Their membership has become increasingly important as their numbers grow; first, because they are becoming more important in the global economy, and second, because trade is often the vital tool in their development efforts. The world's developing countries are a highly diverse group with very different views and concerns, so it is not always easy to reach an agreement.

The WTO assists developing countries in three ways:

1. Many WTO agreements include numerous provisions giving developing and least-developed countries special rights or extra leniency.

2. The WTO Secretariat has special legal advisers for assisting developing countries in any WTO dispute and for giving them legal counsel.

3. The WTO provides extensive education and technical assistance to countries with developing markets, helping them draft laws and implement policies favorable to trade.

Pictured here is a branch of the Bank of Brazil in Rio de Janerio. The IMF helps to smooth out fluctuations in currency values and to stabilize the buying power of consumers in countries across the world.

The United Nations works very closely with the WTO to help developing countries. In October 1997, six international organizations including the IMF, the International Trade Centre, the United Nations Conference for Trade and Development, the UNDP, the World Bank, and the WTO launched the Integrated Framework, a joint technical assistance program exclusively for the world's least-developed countries. It was reviewed in 2005, when the Enhanced Integrated Framework was adopted.

* * *

Although aid is available in many forms and from many sources, the situation in much of the developing world remains grim. Far from the wealth and luxury of the Western world, people struggle daily with issues such as poverty, hunger, illiteracy, and disease. As the world's only truly global body, the United Nations has a special obligation to bring the needs of the world's most vulnerable to the attention of those with the means to help. Through its extensive network of official agencies, its power to affect its own extensive membership, and through cooperation with international institutions and aid agencies, the United Nations is committed to meeting the challenges of development around the globe.

CHAPTER FIVE

TEXT-DEPENDENT QUESTIONS

1. Explain what ODA is and where it comes from.

2. How does the World Bank help developing nations?

3. How does the WTO help developing nations?

RESEARCH PROJECTS

1. Research and write a report on how the World Trade Organization helps expand globalization.

2. Research a list of the projects the World Bank has helped fund. Pick one of those projects and use the Internet and library to gather news clippings on that particular project. Compile the headlines from those clippings in a journal and write a short summation of what happened.

TIME LINE

1944   The United Nations Monetary and Financial Conference is held in Bretton Woods, New Hampshire.

1945   The United Nations officially comes into existence.

1945   The World Bank institutions and the IMF are officially incorporated.

1965   The UNDP is established.

1972   The United Nations issues the Stockholm Declaration.

1990   The United Nations issues the first Human Development Report.

1990   The Human Development Index (HDI) is developed by Pakistani economist Mahbub ul Haq.

1992   The United Nations holds the Rio Earth Summit; it unveils Agenda 21.

1992   The Commission on Sustainable Development is established.

1993   The Human Development Report begins to use the HDI to rank countries.

1997   The General Assembly holds special "Rio+5" session to review progress toward implementing Agenda 21.

2000	The Millennium Summit takes place, and Millennium Development Goals are established.
2002	The World Summit on Sustainable Development is held in Johannesburg, South Africa.
2002	The International Conference on Financing for Development is held in Monterrey, Mexico.
2005	The Beijing Declaration on Renewable Energy for Sustainable Development is issued.
2006	The Rio+20 conference convenes and renews the UN's commitment to sustainable development.
2014	The United Nations General Assembly unanimously declares 2014–2024 as the Decade of Sustainable Energy for All.
2015	The United Nations leads the international community in preparing a new development agenda as the target date for the Millennium Development Goals is reached.

FURTHER RESEARCH

Books

Collin, Robin Morris, and Robert William Collin. *Encyclopedia of Sustainability*. Westport, CT: Greenwood, 2009.

Cooper, Phillip J., and Claudia María Vargas. *Sustainable Development in Crisis Conditions: Challenges of War, Terrorism, and Civil Disorder*. Lanham, MD: Rowman and Littlefield, 2007.

Report of the World Social Situation: Inequality Matters. New York: United Nations, 2013.

Report of the World Social Situation: Rethinking Poverty. New York: United Nations, 2010.

Online Sources

Development Gateway: www.developmentgateway.org

Global Policy Forum: www.globalpolicy.org

International Monetary Fund: www.imf.org/external/

The World Bank: www.worldbank.org

World Trade Organization: www.wto.org

UNDP Human Development Report 2014
hdr.undp.org/en/content/human-development-report-2014

United Nations Development Program: www.undp.org

NOTE TO EDUCATORS: This book contains both imperial and metric measurements as well as references to global practices and trends in an effort to encourage the student to gain a worldly perspective. We, as publishers, feel it's our role to give young adults the tools they need to thrive in a global society.

SERIES GLOSSARY

abstain: not to vote for or against proposal when a vote is held.

Allies: the countries that fought against Germany in World War I or against the Axis powers in World War II.

ambassador: an official representative of one country to another country.

amendments: process of changing a legal document.

appeal: a formal request to a higher authority requesting a change of a decision.

appeasement: a deliberate attempt pacify a potentially troublesome nation.

arbitration: the process of resolving disputes through an impartial third party.

asylum: protection granted by a nation to someone who has left fled their country as a political refugee.

Axis: the alliance of Germany, Italy, and Japan that fought the allies in World War II.

blocs: groups of countries or political parties with the same goal.

bureaucracy: a complex system of administration, usually of a government or corporation.

capital: material wealth in the form of money or property.

civil law: law of a state dealing with the rights of private citizens.

coalition: in military terms, a group of nations joined together for a common purpose against a common enemy.

codification: the arrangement of laws into a systematic code.

Cold War: a largely nonviolent conflict between capitalist and communist countries following World War II.

compliance: conforming to a regulation or law.

conservation: preservation, management, and care of natural and cultural resources.

constitution: an official document outlining the rules of a system or government.

conventions: agreements between countries, less formal than treaties.

decolonization: the act of granting a colony its independence.

delegates: individuals chosen to represent or act on behalf of an organization or government.

demographic: characteristics of a human population.

diplomatic: having to do with international negotiations without resorting to violence.

disarmament: the reduction of a nation's supply of weapons or strength of its armed forces.

due process: the official procedures in legal cases required by law to ensure that the rights of all people involves are protected.

embargo: a government order limiting or prohibiting trade.

envoys: diplomats who act on behalf of a national government.

epidemic: a widespread occurrence of an infectious disease.

ethnic cleansing: the killing or imprisonment of an ethnic minority by a dominant group.

exchange rates: rates at which money of one country is exchanged the money of another.

extradition: the handing over by one government of someone accused of a crime in a different country for trial or punishment.

extremist: having to do with radical political or religious beliefs.

factions: smaller groups within larger groups that have opposing ideas.

fascist: relating to a system of government characterized by dictatorship, repression of opposition, and extreme nationalism.

flashpoints: areas of intense conflict and insecurity that often erupt into violent confrontation.

forgery: the act of making or producing an illegal copy of something.

free-market economy: economic system in which businesses operate without government control in matters such as pricing and wage levels.

genocide: systematic killing of all people from a national, ethnic, or religious group, or an attempt to do so.

globalization: the various processes that increase connections peoples of the world.

gross domestic product: total value of all goods and services produced within a country.

guerrilla: unorganized and small-scale warfare carried out by independent units.

human trafficking: the practice of seizing people against their will for the purpose of "selling" them for work, usually in the sex trade.

humanitarian: being concerned with or wanting to promote the well-being of other humans.

ideological: based on a specific system of beliefs, values, and ideas forming the basis of a social, economic, or political philosophy

indigenous: relating to the original inhabitants of an area or environment.

infrastructure: physical structures of a region, made up of roads, bridges, and so forth.

isolationism: the belief that a country should limit their involvement in the affairs of other countries.

mandate: an official instruction by an authority.

mediation: the process of resolving a dispute.

money laundering: the transferring of illegally obtained money through various businesses and accounts so as to hide it.

nationalists: people with an extreme sense of loyalty to their country.

nationalize: takeover by a government of a private business.

pandemic: a widespread epidemic in which a disease spreads to many countries and regions of the world.

per capita income: average amount earned by each individual in a country.

preamble: introduction, or opening words of a document.

precedent: established practice; a decision used as the basis of future decisions.

proliferation: the rapid spread of something.

propaganda: information or publicity put out by an organization or government to spread and promote a policy or idea.

protocols: preliminary memoranda often formulated and signed by diplomatic negotiators.

rapporteur: an official in charge of investigating and reporting to an agency, institution, or other entity.

ratification: the act of formally approving something.

referendum: a vote of the entire electorate on a question or questions put before it by the government or similar body.

reparation: compensation made by a nation defeated by others in a war.

sanction: a punishment imposed as a result of breaking a rule or law.

signatories: persons or governments who have signed a treaty and are bound by it.

sovereignty: self-rule, usually of a nation.

standard of living: the minimum amount of necessities essential to maintaining a comfortable life.

summit: a meeting between heads of government or other high-ranking officials.

sustainable: able to be maintained so that the resource is not depleted or damaged.

veto: the power of a person, country, or branch of government to reject the legislation of another.

INDEX

PICTURE CREDITS

Page	Location	Archive/Photographer
8	Middle	Wikimedia Commons/Rachel
11	Top	Wikimedia Commons/Albert Backer
12-13	Spread	Flickr/MONUSCO; Denise Maheho
15	Top	Wikimedia Commons/U.S. Agency for International Development
16	Bottom	Wikimedia Commons/SuSanA Secretariat
18	Top	Wikimedia Commons/United Nations Development Programme
19	Bottom	Flickr/UNIDO
20	Middle	Wikimedia Commons/Kate Dixon
22	Top	Wikimedia Commons/Sebastiaan ter Burg
24	Middle	Wikimedia Commons/Vmenkov
26-27	Top	iStock.com/lopurice
29	Full page	Wikimedia Commons/Cristian Bortes
33	Full page	Wikimedia Commons/U.S. Fish & Wildlife Service
34	Full page	Wikimedia Commons/DVIDSHUB
37	Full page	Wikimedia Commons/Alpha du centaure
38	Full page	Wikimedia Commons/Kendra Helmer, USAID
41	Top	Flickr/UNIDO
42	Bottom	Public Domain
44	Bottom	Wikimedia Commons/UNCTAD
46	Middle	Wikimedia Commons/Nick Carson
48	Bottom	Public Domain
51	Top	Wikimedia Commons/IICD
52	Top	Wikimedia Commons/SuSanA Secretariat
53	Bottom	Wikimedia Commons/Husond
54	Middle	Wikimedia Commons/Michael Gäbler
56	Top	Wikimedia Commons/Anajur
58	Middle	Wikimedia Commons/Department of Foreign Affairs and Trade
60-61	Bottom	Wikimedia Commons/Freedom's Falcon
63	Top	Public Domain
66	Bottom	Wikimedia Commons/David Rydevik
68	Middle	Wikimedia Commons/UK Department for International Development
71	Top	Wikimedia Commons/Willem Heerbaart
72	Bottom	Dollar Photo Club/vvoe
74	Full page	Wikimedia Commons/William Cho
76	Top	Wikimedia Commons/Eduardo P

BIOGRAPHIES

Author

HEATHER DOCALAVICH first became interested in the work of the United Nations while working as an adviser for a high school Model UN program. She lives in Hilton Head Island, South Carolina, with her four children.

Series Advisor

BRUCE RUSSETT is Dean Acheson Professor of Political Science at Yale University and editor of the Journal of Conflict Resolution. He has taught or researched at Columbia, Harvard, M.I.T., Michigan, and North Carolina in the United States, and educational institutions in Belgium, Britain, Israel, Japan, and the Netherlands. He has been president of the International Studies Association and the Peace Science Society, and holds an honorary doctorate from Uppsala University in Sweden. He was principal adviser to the U.S. Catholic Bishops for their pastoral letter on nuclear deterrence in 1985, and codirected the staff for the 1995 Ford Foundation report, *The United Nations in Its Second Half Century*. He has served as editor of the *Journal of Conflict Resolution* since 1973. The twenty-five books he has published include *The Once and Future Security Council* (1997), *Triangulating Peace: Democracy, Interdependence, and International Organizations* (2001), *World Politics: The Menu for Choice* (8th edition 2006), and *Purpose and Policy in the Global Community* (2006).